God Made A Believer Out of Me

Kimberly Robinson

Copyright © 2021 by **Kimberly Robinson**

All rights reserved. No part of this publication may be reproduced, distributed or transmitted in any form or by any means, including photocopying, recording, or other electronic or mechanical methods, without the prior written permission of the publisher, except in the case of brief quotations embodied in critical reviews and certain other noncommercial uses permitted by copyright law. For permission requests, write to the publisher, addressed "Attention: Permissions Coordinator," at the address below.

Kimberly Robinson/Rejoice Essential Publishing

PO BOX 512

Effingham, SC 29541

www.republishing.org

Unless otherwise indicated, scripture is taken from the King James Version.'

The Holy Bible, English Standard Version® (ESV®) Copyright © 2001 by Crossway, a publishing ministry of Good News Publishers. All rights reserved. ESV Text Edition: 2016

God Made A Believer Out of Me/Kimberly Robinson

ISBN-13: 978-1-952312-88-5

LCCN: 2021916629

Dedication

FIRST AND FOREMOST, I wanted to dedicate my book to God.

Thank you to my wonderful mother, Ethel Robinson, and my two brothers Garlan and David Robinson.

My seven beautiful children are Gabriell, Raphael, Sebastian Robinson and Precious, Serenity, Nehemiah, and Annastasia Williams. I love you all.

To Apostle Ken Cox, my spiritual dad and his wife, Sabina Cox, Apostle Willie Rhames, my spiritual mom and spiritual brother Curtis Gause, thank you for encouraging me to write the books God has placed inside me.

Thank you all for believing in me and for being here for me and all your support.

TABLE OF CONTENTS

INTRODUCTION..1

CHAPTER ONE: My Early Lifestyle............6

CHAPTER TWO: My Life With Michael..10

CHAPTER THREE: The Torment of My Life...................................15

CHAPTER FOUR: My Encounter With God..................................20

CHAPTER FIVE My Motivation To Serve God......................28

ABOUT THE AUTHOR...32

INTRODUCTION

I have had many moments in my life where I questioned God, not understanding why I was ever created, searching for a meaning for existing. I was empty on the inside. I was trying to fill myself with things and people, only to remain empty. My cup was not half full. It was dry. I learned that people are seeking two things in life. That is who they are and why they are here. I was trying to go around a mountain that was too wide to go around and too high to climb. One day God said, "I never told you to go around the mountain. I never told you to climb the mountain. I told you to speak to the mountain and tell the mountain to move." Yet my biggest problem was not speaking to the mountain nor casting it into the sea. It is what came after that I could not seem to grasp. For so long, God says, "We shall

God Made A Believer Out of Me

not doubt in our heart but shall believe those things which He saith shall come to pass and we shall have whatsoever He saith."

This takes a tremendous amount of faith if you ask me. I did not have a mustard seed. I refused to believe because what I saw was what I believed. Everything around me was in constant chaos. I could not sort through all of that. I was hearing the voice of God during my chaos leading me and directing my steps, teaching me how to maneuver through life-threatening situations. In my distress, I cried unto the Lord, and He heard me. My enemies were like an army against me. However, God encamped a host of angels around me. No matter where I went, He was with me. He promised never to leave me nor forsake me.

I found myself in strange cities and states being led by my addiction to crack cocaine. Running from the drugs, not knowing I was taking me with me. No matter where I ended up, I got high. I repeated the cycle all over again. Drugs, prostitution, and losing everything repeatedly are a part of my story. No matter the loss, I am

INTRODUCTION

still here by God's grace and mercy. I found favor with the God of Abraham, Isaac, and Jacob. He is the true and living God. Having been chosen from my mother's womb, God said He knew my life was predestined from the foundations of this world. It is the process in between that most of us struggle to understand. I was questioning the God who knows all and is all and is the in-between. He is the Alpha and Omega, the beginning and the end, and the first and the last. He is the author and finisher of my faith. He is the one that began a good work in me that shall finish it until the day of Christ. Jesus sits at the right hand of the Father, and He makes intercession for me. He said He would put no more on me than I can bear.

I have fought many battles and witnessed many miracles. I have seen many giants fall. I wrestle not against flesh and blood but against principalities, against powers, against the rulers of the darkness of this world, against spiritual wickedness in high places. The whole armour of God allows me to stand against the wiles of the devil. I cannot say that I was prepared for such a fight; however, I certainly learned how to maneuver in the fight. The streets prepared me. I learned how to watch and study people. I learned how to survive in the worst of situations. After coming into the Kingdom of God, I studied the enemy and learned his tactics. It is hard to win a fight if you do not know your opponent. Little did I know that God was training me. I did not realize that He gave me the weaponry needed for the constant battles I was facing. I never knew that the greatness of my life called for such a fight. I was often exhausted, and I wanted to give up, and at times I gave in, but God kept me through it all. His grace was sufficient for me. I never knew God was so merciful until I kept messing up repeatedly. I felt like a failure you would not believe. But that is what the devil wanted me to feel. He is the accuser of the brethren. I learned that this is not about how I feel, it is about what God said about me. Until I lined up with those facts and began to speak the word over my life, nothing really changed. I had to change my circumstances with my mouth.

Proverbs 18:21 says, "Death and life are in the power of the tongue: and they that love it shall eat the fruit thereof."

INTRODUCTION

Proverbs 18:20 says, "A man's belly shall be satisfied with the fruit of his lips and with the increase of his lips shall he be filled."

Kimberly Robinson
6601 Newbury Way
Wilmington, N.C. 28411
(910) 386-9851
Kimberlytateel@gmail.com.

CHAPTER ONE

My Early Lifestyle

MY PROCESS WITH GOD began during a full-blown addiction to crack cocaine. I had to be in my early thirties. The Spirit of the Lord began to draw me from the dark place I was into His marvelous light. I found myself being led into churches in my area, unaware of what was transpiring in my life. I was so lost, blind, full of anger, disappointment, unforgiveness, and bitterness. All I knew was that I did not want to die a crack addict. Something on the inside of me was thirsty and hungry for a better life. I was so used to failure and disappointment that it became a mechanism or a way I survived. I hid inside myself.

My Early Lifestyle

Satan temporarily took my voice through sexual abuse at the age of six. Having found my way of escape through drugs when I was seventeen, I would have never found my voice. As silly as it may sound, drugs brought me out of myself. I began to talk about the abuse and the emotional pain it was causing me. I was first locked up in a mental prison before addiction led me to be incarcerated repeatedly. Life seems to be passing me by, and all hope seems lost for me. I remember days I would just talk to the God that my mother and grandmother knew. I did not know Him for myself. I have to say there was nothing I did or could have done to find God. He found me. He drew me then began to clean me up. My life was a mess. I was so broken. I wanted to believe that this God was real. At that time, I did not understand why a loving God did not protect me from that pervert or why He would allow so many terrible things to happen to me. I had so many questions for God, and all I wanted was answers and retribution for all the men that hurt me through sexual abuse, sexual assault, and physical abuse.

God Made A Believer Out of Me

I even had one pimp me out for two years on a military base every day. He would beat the mess out of me. I never saw a dime of the money. I left home when I was seventeen. I was tired of that man touching me and having sex with me. There was a strain on my relationship with my mother. She could not see what was going on, and I was afraid to tell her because he threatened to kill my family and me. Of course, I believed him. I hated my mom because I thought that she knew and chose not to protect me. For her to be an overprotective parent, I just did not understand. The devil was telling me that she hated me. One night I heard the devil say, "Go and kill your mother." I went downstairs, got a knife, went into her bedroom, and stood over her with the knife when a small still voice said, "Do not do it." I quietly left the room, went back upstairs, and was tormented all night long.

One night I was lying in bed when I saw an image of something creepy in my window, and I ran downstairs to get my mother. I was scared and crying. My mother did not get up. However, she sent her boyfriend at that time upstairs to see what I was talking about. He said he did not see

My Early Lifestyle

anything. I pleaded with him. "It is right there," I said. They thought I was crazy, but I know what I saw. I refuse to leave them alone about it, so my mother's boyfriend nailed the window shut so it could never open. She was still friends with the perpetrator, so he came around all the time.

CHAPTER TWO

My Life With Michael

AFTER LEAVING HOME AT 17, I ended up in jail for the second time for prostitution. I was 16 when I got caught for the first time shoplifting in Rose's with a friend. Oh, did the people talk about me? I was young with a bad reputation. How do you redeem yourself from such a name? "She's a whore." I am now known for being easy. I had already given birth to my first child Gabriell who my mother raised at the time. I met a man named Michael. I was not attracted to him. It was something about him that I did not like. One night I saw him at a dance, and the next thing I remember, I was waking up beside him in his bed naked, and I could tell he had sex with me. He drugged me because I was homeless, and I ended up living with him and his mother. It was not long before the abuse started. I ended up pregnant again. Michael tried to kill me when I was in my later pregnancy. He was dragging me up and down the street. He took a rock and carved it into my skin, threw a set of weights on me, blacked both of my eyes, and beat me with a broomstick. The beating went on for hours. My unborn child was a miracle to be alive after that day. Michael was very jealous and possessive, so he made me think I was wrong when I was not. Him beating me and cheating on me was my fault. He had so many other girlfriends. Every time I turned around, some female was approaching me to fight over him. I had to fight over my man. Another woman and me were pregnant at the same time. Our children were born a month apart. I gave birth to a son named Raphael. Getting away from this man was not easy.

Then one day, Michael was killed, and I was left with a son to raise all by myself. I did get housing, and the party life began. I was drinking heavily, and then the night came when I was

God Made A Believer Out of Me

introduced to crack cocaine. I was 19 years old. At first, I remember feeling nothing until I hit it again. I cannot explain the euphoria and what set off into my brain. I fell in love. It was not long before I was falling deeper and deeper into darkness. Before I knew it, I was getting high in crack houses, abandoned houses, the woods, and sometimes out in the open streets. My addiction led me into places against my own will. I was hopping in and out of cars selling my body to get high. Over time I realized I was no longer getting high; I was getting low. I could not take care of my kids. It was not long before I was pregnant with child number three. Sadly, to say I was getting high the entire nine months of pregnancy. Three days before I went into labor, a still small voice said, "Don't get high for three days." One thing about the still, small voice, I obeyed it. After the third day, I went into labor and had another son named Sebastian. The devil had a trap set, but God had a plan for my life. Even though I could not see the plan at the time, God protected me.

Many times, I was physically abused by so many men. I must admit I hated men. They took advantage of me. They preyed on my weakness for drugs. Because I was fared to look upon, I was treated like a piece of meat. One of the deceptions the enemy used was the man that sexually abused me paid me for the sex he took from me. I equated sex and money together. I also equated that as love. For years I was confused. I did not know who I was. I did not know my purpose and was searching for my identity. I became so confused that I began to date women. The women I dated turned out to be like the men, abusive. I was looking for love in all the wrong places. However, the sad part is love. I had nothing to go by. I did not know what love looked like. People were judging me without knowing my story. Nobody knew what I was really going through or endured.

My mother was divorced. My father was not around. I never shared with my own family that I was raped at 13 by a boy in high school. After school, I was walking up to my back porch to go into the house. When I put the key in the door and opened it, he came up from nowhere so fast, pushed me in the backdoor, and raped me right there on the kitchen floor. He had to be watching me for a while to know that I went straight home after school every day and was usually there by myself until after five. My mother worked a full-time job and raised three children alone, so I went home and cooked every day and kept the house clean. I also made sure my homework was done. My brothers got to hang out with their friends. I did not get to enjoy my childhood or teenage years. That was happening along with being molested at the same time. I ended up being pregnant, not knowing which one was the unborn baby's father. I was so young and naive that I didn't realize I was carrying a baby in my belly.

I was standing in the dining room yawning and stretching when my mom asked, "Girl, are you pregnant?" She was looking at my stomach. All I could say was, "No momma." She felt my stomach and said, "You're pregnant." My stomach was hard. I did not even feel anything moving around in there.

CHAPTER THREE

The Torment of My Life

MY MOTHER TOOK ME to two doctors. First, to confirm that I was pregnant and because I was further than my first trimester to be able to get an abortion in the city I lived in. She took me to a clinic in Jacksonville. I was told I was too far along to have an abortion, but the clinic in Jacksonville, NC, gave me one anyway. As it turned out, I was seven and a half months pregnant. They killed a live fetus. Truth be told, that is the day everything inside of me died. It felt as if the baby was running inside me, trying to escape the long instrument used to kill the baby. Afterwards, a machine suctioned it out. As I laid there traumatized, I remember feeling so numb.

God Made A Believer Out of Me

I was in shock. As young as I was, I wanted to have my baby because I wanted someone to love me. I was so empty on the inside. I did not want to live anymore. I tried to commit suicide for the first time when I was 17. I took a whole lot of pills hoping that would be the end for me. I ended up on the 7th floor in the hospital, a psychiatric ward because I was already cutting myself. I remember hating the fact that it did not work.

I was diagnosed with borderline personality disorder and Post Traumatic Stress Disorder or PTSD. I had been having nightmares and wetting the bed for many years now; then, I started having panic attacks at 19 years old. These attacks lasted for many years without treatment. Panic attacks were the scariest thing a person could ever experience. They would happen when I was least expected. They got so bad I could not drive. These attacks and drugs did not go together. It feels like you have a heart attack, except that what you are experiencing is not even real. A medical doctor told me that. It had to be God because there is no other way to explain how I did not lose my mind. I remember many things triggering panic attacks like police sirens, the

The Torment of My Life

EMS, or any loud noises. Fear certainly had a grip on my life. Here I am, a grown woman living in my first apartment, and I would stay up all night because I was afraid someone would break in and hurt me. I kept all the lights on in the house and the television. However, I would have the tv where you could not hear the sound. I only needed the light. I would fall asleep as soon as daylight appeared. Sometimes, I would be so tired I would fall asleep accidentally in the night. But if I did, the night hag would always ride me. I did not know what a night hag was until my grandmother told me. I fought the night hag for many years. I would hallucinate and hear voices.

During this time, I started drinking alcohol heavily so I could sleep. Even though I was drinking, I would still try to stay up all night. I was scared all the time. Often, I would see images of darkness or demons. They visited me all the time. I thought I was crazy. My biggest fight began with the spirit world. I was not aware I was battling with the spiritual realm and that the enemy was trying to assassinate me. He was after me from the womb. He was after my mind, this book, my testimony, and my voice. He knew

God Made A Believer Out of Me

that if I ever got free, what God could do with me. Who can testify with me that his plan did not work?

Jeremiah 1:5 (ESV) says, "Before I formed you in the womb I knew you, and before you were born I consecrated you; I appointed you a prophet to the nations." Looking back over the fight I was in, I could see the hand of God. God's hand was all over me. He chose me for such a time as this to minister to other people who are lost and dying. I know how pain feels. Who can better tell a story than someone who has walked through and overcame every obstacle that the enemy has formed against you?

Isaiah 54:17 says, "No weapon that is formed against thee shall prosper, and every tongue that shall rise against thee in judgment thou shalt condemn. This is the heritage of the servants of the Lord, and their righteousness is of Me, saith the Lord."

There was nothing that I could have done to earn God's love. I am His daughter, and He is my heavenly Father who art in heaven. My search was about hunger and thirst for righteousness. I was chosen for this purpose.

Matthew 5:6 says, "Blessed are those that hunger and thirst for righteousness, for they shall be filled."

I learned that when God says something, it shall and will be. He is a promise keeper.

Matthew 19:26 says, "With God, all things are possible."

His promises are not empty.

2 Peter 3:9 says, "The Lord is not slack concerning His promises."

Numbers 23:19 says, "God is not a man, that He should lie; neither the son of man, that He should repent: hath He said, and shall He not do it? Or hath He spoken, and shall He not make it good?"

So far, God has made good on what He has said concerning me.

CHAPTER FOUR

My Encounter With God

Back in December 2009, I lost custody of my children again. By this time, I am a mother of seven, three of which are grown, and my last four children were 5, 8, 9, and 10. Not only did I lose them, but I also had to sign my parental rights away. I was never supposed to get my children back, but God said, "I am going to turn it around." I remember not being able to figure out in my natural mind how God was going to do that thing. I was in constant turmoil. It was a devastating situation. I felt like I was on a roller coaster ride with my faith at the time: one minute trusting what God said and the next minute walking in doubt and unbelief.

My Encounter With God

Three months later, God turned it around, and the way He did it, I would have never expected it. Everybody that was against me turned in my favor. The judge said the case was giving him a headache. He could not understand why everyone turned in my favor. Mind you, I was not doing what the judge recommended me to do. In fact, I had done just the opposite. I had got married and was in an abusive marriage. I remember the enemy using this man to intimidate me until one day, I stood up to the spirit using him and had a restraining order taken out on him and had him removed from our home. Well, that very same day, he had me arrested because he knew that I had an outstanding warrant for my arrest. I went to jail, but God had been faithful because I was in a strange town with no family there. God already had the people in place to help me through everything. I stayed in jail a few days before I was bonded out. I had an evangelist friend who watched my children for one night and then took them to their brother's house in Durham.

God Made A Believer Out of Me

When I got out of jail, this man had the lights and water turned off. He took the food and my Bible. He knew how much I read the Bible. I was not capable of meeting his requirements at that time in my life. I didn't need to be with a man who wasn't in any way going to help but become a problem. I still struggled back and forth with substance use. Even though the Lord had found me, and the process had begun, I was learning the things of God. I was learning how God operates, His nature. He was demonstrating His love for me and His power at the same time. I just had to pay attention because the class was in session. I was passing and failing. Some things I repeatedly failed, especially with intimate relationships and drugs. I was learning where I was in the process. I realized I am a slow learner. I had attachment and abandonment issues. These two struggles were hard for me to let go of. I did not give up though. I kept trying and continued praying.

God revealed I killed the relationship the moment I had sex with a person. Sex before marriage clouds our judgment. You will spend too much time on something that has no life in it.

It is already dead. I call this Spiritual Russian Roulette.

James 1:15 says, "Then when desire has conceived, it gives birth to sin; and sin when it is full-grown, brings forth death."

I repeated this cycle over and again. I kept falling short in this area because of the sexual abuse. I did not love myself. It was a process of loving me.

God was faithful in showing me that I am His child and that He loved me in spite of me. He kept giving me a reason to believe in His existence. He looked beyond my faults and saw my needs. I never overlooked my faults and failures. God brought me to a place of accountability. I was always honest with Him. I talked to God about all my struggles. I did not act as if the struggles were not there. I remember when the shift took place, even though I had a relationship with God and by this time full of the Word, I did not believe the Word I was preaching to others. I cried out unto God one day, and I asked Him why He wouldn't punish all the men that had hurt me? What God said to me that day changed my whole perspective. He said, "Because I want to deal with you about you." He revealed to me through a picture on the wall by saying, "Look at that picture and tell me what you see," and I looked at it. I said, "I see a beautiful flower." Then He said, "If five people in a room look at the same picture, everyone would say and see something different. It's a whole picture. Take the men out of the equation and look at your part. What part do you play?" I realized that I was my biggest problem. Here is where blaming other people stopped for me. God already knows the heart of man. So, I willingly confessed my struggles with Him. I certainly did not have the power to lay down every sin and weight that so easily beset me. Relationships were my downfall. For years, I thought it was the drugs alone until the Lord revealed that it starts with the man, leading to the drugs.

You attract what you are, and I was a dressed-up garbage can. I looked good on the outside, but the inside was filthy, dirty, and stinky. I ended up with filthy, dirty, stinky men. I am referring to the heart as well as the soul. Until some years ago, I was physically abused by every man I had ever been in a relationship with. God was processing me through the pain I had been experiencing in my life. What's really crazy is I wanted every man to be the one. The right one, and for a long time, I did not know what the right one looked like either. No matter how abusive he was. I was a sick individual. Each time he never was. I thought I was drinking from two wells. I would be so disappointed. Thinking I had something each time, but it was the same man; he just had a different face and name. I was so needy when it came to a man. Not sure if I was looking for the father I never had or what. Loving God for me was not easy, nor was trusting Him. He was still a man to me. He had to prove Himself.

God was still faithful, and He never walked away. Every time I called on Him, He was there. Sometimes I did not have to call on Him; He would rescue me in spite of me. I had gotten myself in situations I know only God delivered me out of. I could be dead. I could be doing a life sentence in prison. I could be HIV positive. I in no way look like what I have been through. I could be in a mental institution, not knowing who I am. Better yet, I could still be addicted to crack, fornicating, and living in sin, but God pulled me out all the way. He would not allow any of the relationships I was in work. Some really hurt, and I struggled with "Why God?" I no longer question Him; I trust it is for my good. The majority was a thank you, God, if I can be honest. None of the men I was with even deserved my time or to be in my presence. God was doing for me what I could not seem to do for myself. I hated choosing men over God. I could not sleep with a man without feeling convicted because I belong to God. My heartfelt love for God would not allow me to have peace. He loved me enough not to let me have what I thought I wanted.

Looking back, I do not know what I was thinking. I was choosing to lose every time. Of course, the devil made me think I was missing out on something when I was actually not. I learned the hard way that the Word of God worked whether I believed it or not. It is called the law of the universe. I do not believe that I wasted time since all things work together for my good with God. He is turning my mess into a message. He has been that faithful rock in proving Himself. He told me that He was going to use me because I am real. He said you would only have to speak it and it will be so. God knows I know how to be transparent. I cannot be anything else other than what God is calling me to be. I was looking back over my life, and I realized how far He had brought me, and I am in awe of what God can and does. When He says no one else will get the glory, He means it. I sit with my God allowing the Holy Spirit to lead me. So many times, I wanted to admit defeat and give up on life. Every time I thought I would give up, a new strength came until my next relationship. I kept doing the same thing over and over, expecting a different result.

CHAPTER FIVE

My Motivation To Serve God

*I*NSANITY, THAT IS WHAT that is. I married for the third time, once again believing I had something. Now I thought he was the one. He was my best friend, so I thought. He was my brother in the Lord. There were some differences in our relationship. However, I was chalking them up as flaws, and we all have them. I mean, no two people are alike. We went through spiritual marriage counseling with our Pastor. The Pastor had us write a pros and cons list, and we both decided that we could live with our differences. All relationships take work, and we were willing to do the work.

My Motivation To Serve God

Nothing at that time really seemed major until it all hit the fan. Nine months in, he left me for another woman: the same woman he left his first wife and children for. He turned out to be the monster of them all. I am ashamed to talk about all this man did to my daughter and me. I kept expecting God to bless my mess. We were not abstinent before marriage. I thought I would lose my mind after this because everything happened so fast and unexpectedly. This was my motivation to do things completely God's way. No more drugs, no more sex before marriage. If only I could keep my legs close for two minutes, who knows what would happen. I did not respect my body, so why would he or any man.

I dated abusive men and married them because I did not want to live in sin, but I did not want to be alone. I did truly love my last husband. Whatever I was looking for in a man, I did not find it. I finally surrendered to the will of God fully for my life. God's love is enough. God is enough. He has proven himself to me through being faithful, loving, kind, and patient. I could have never made it without God. I could have been dead many times over. God is still here when every known man is gone, been gone. Now I understand grace and mercy. I am worthy. Being alone is not so bad after all. I do not have to answer to anyone except God. Now, I can do some things for myself and by myself. I decided to trade in my old life for the new life in Christ Jesus. For I know the plans I have for you, says the Lord. His plans are of good and not of evil to give me a future and a hope and to bring me to an expected end (Jeremiah 29:11).

I am learning how to be okay with myself and to be alone. Self-love is the best love. Greater love hath no man than this than to lay down his life for his friends (John 15:13). Jesus certainly laid down His life for me so that I might have life and that more abundantly. God made a believer out of me. "And being fully persuaded that, what He had promised, He was able to perform (Romans 4:21)." I thank God that I have been a witness to many miracles and so many supernatural encounters. Nobody can't convince me that God is not who He says He is. He is the King of Kings and Lord of Lords. He is omnipotent, omniscience, and omnipresent. He is the author and finisher of my faith. He is the living word. I can

My Motivation To Serve God

go on and on about God because I love Him, and He is amazing; He is awesome in all his ways. He chastises those whom He loves. His correction hurts, but it is out of love. He knows what is best for me.

I finally plan to spend the rest of my days serving Him for real. I know my purpose, and I am more than grateful that God chose me for this assignment. I am more than grateful for the process, for it has taught me much and has allowed me to see just how great God is. I owe Him my life. There was a time when I could not see, nor did I believe that my life would be the way it is now. I repent wholeheartedly for putting my faith, hope, and trust in another human being. I pray many blessings upon the readers of my book, and I encourage you to get up and do something amazing. You are gifted, and God needs you. The body of Christ needs your gifts. People are waiting on you and only you: blessings, my dear friends.

About The Author

KIMBERLY SPENT A LARGE portion of her life addicted to crack cocaine and incarcerated. Her criminal history goes back to when she was in high school. After her last marriage, she decided to go all the way with God. Between 2005 and 2006, she fell away from God. She was on fire for God but chose to go back to the streets and get high after being clean for at least nine years. She realized that it was anger and unbelief toward God that resulted from past hurt. She wanted God to punish all the men that had left her broken and scarred. She did not understand that in God's timing, people will come to repentance and reap what they sow. She learned that

About The Author

God deals with you as an individual. It wasn't until she cried out to God that it changed her perception. She then was able to start looking at herself and be accountable for her wrong while forgiving and learning to love all over again. This brought freedom from all the trauma she endured in the past and confidence.

God was so faithful in making a believer out of her. She has come to know a love that no man has ever given. Her life is filled with thankfulness to God for delivering and keeping her when she did not want to be kept. After three attempts to commit suicide and cutting herself from the age of sixteen until 2007, nobody can make her deny that God is not who He says He is. Her deliverance was not instant but for sure. Today, she can declare and testify that "I Am A Believer."

Index

A

abandoned houses, 12
abandonment issues, 22
abortion, 15
Abraham, 3
abusive marriage, 21
accountability, 23
accountable, 33
accuser of the brethren, 4
addiction, 2, 6, 7, 12
afraid, 8, 17
Alpha, 3
angels, 2
anger, 6, 32
apartment, 17
arrested, 21
ashamed, 29
assassinate, 17
assignment, 31

Index

attracted, 10
author, 3, 30

B

baby, 14, 15, 16
back porch, 13
backdoor, 13
battles, 3, 4
beautiful flower, 24
bed, 8, 10, 16
bedroom, 8
believe, 2, 4, 7, 23, 26, 31
belly, 5, 14
Bible, 22
bitterness, 6
Blessed, 19
blind, 6
book, 17, 31
borderline personality disorder, 16
boyfriend, 8, 9
brain, 12
broken, 7, 32
broomstick, 11
brothers, 14

C

cars, 12
chaos, 2
cheating, 11
child, 10, 11, 12, 23
childhood, 14
children, 11, 14, 20, 21, 29
Christ, 3, 30, 31
churches, 6
cities, 2
class, 22
clinic, 15
condemn, 18
confidence, 33
confused, 13
cons, 28
consecrated, 18
convicted, 26
correction, 31
crack addict, 6
crack cocaine, 2, 6, 12, 32
crack houses, 12
crazy, 9, 17, 25
created, 1
criminal history, 32

Index

crying, 8
cup, 1
custody, 20

D

dance, 10
darkness, 3, 12, 17
daughter, 18, 29
death, 23
Death, 4
deceptions, 13
defeat, 27
deliverance, 33
desire, 23
devil, 3, 4, 8, 12, 26
dining room, 14
dirty, 24
disappointment, 6
distress, 2
divorced, 13
doctors, 15
door, 13
doubt, 2, 20
downfall, 24
downstairs, 8

drugs, 2, 7, 13, 16, 22, 24, 29
Durham, 21

E

emotional pain, 7
empty, 1, 16, 19
EMS, 17
encourage, 31
enemies, 2
evangelist friend, 21
eyes, 11

F

failure, 4, 6
failures, 23
faith, 2, 3, 20, 30, 31
faithful, 21, 23, 25, 27, 29, 33
family, 8, 13, 21
father, 13, 14, 25
Father, 3, 18
favor, 3, 21
female, 11
fetus, 15
fight, 3, 4, 11, 17, 18

Index

filthy, 24
first trimester, 15
food, 22
forgiving, 33
fornicating, 26
freedom, 33
friends, 9, 14, 30, 31
fruit, 4, 5
future, 30

G

garbage can, 24
giants, 3
gifted, 31
gifts, 31
girlfriends, 11
glory, 27
God, 1, 2, 3, 4, 6, 7, 12, 16, 18, 19, 20, 21, 22, 23, 24, 25, 26, 27, 28, 29, 30, 31, 32, 33
grace, 3, 4, 30
grandmother, 7, 17
grasp, 1
grateful, 31

H

hallucinate, 17
hated, 8, 12, 26
headache, 21
heart, 2, 16, 24
heaven, 18
heritage, 18
high school, 13, 32
HIV positive, 25
Holy Spirit, 27
homeless, 11
homework, 14
honest, 23, 26
hope, 7, 30, 31
hospital, 16
hungry, 6
hurt, 7, 17, 24, 26, 32

I

identity, 13
incarcerated, 7, 32
instrument, 15
intercession, 3
intimate relationships, 22
Isaac, 3

Index

J

Jacob, 3
jail, 10, 21, 22
jealous, 11
Jesus, 3, 30
job, 14
judge, 21
judging, 13
judgment, 18, 22

K

key, 13
kids, 12
kill, 8, 11, 15
Kimberly Robinson, 5
kind, 29
kitchen floor, 13
knife, 8

L

labor, 12

life, 1, 2, 3, 4, 6, 7, 11, 12, 17, 22, 25, 27, 29, 30, 31, 32, 33
lips, 5
Lord, 2, 6, 18, 19, 22, 24, 28, 30
lost, 6, 7, 18, 20
love, 4, 12, 13, 16, 18, 22, 23, 26, 29, 30, 31, 33
loving, 7, 23, 29

M

machine, 15
marriage, 22, 28, 29, 32
mechanism, 6
men, 7, 12, 13, 23, 24, 26, 29, 32
mental institution, 25
mental prison, 7
merciful, 4
mercy, 3, 30
mess, 7, 8, 26, 29
message, 26
Michael, 10, 11
military base, 8
minister, 18
miracles, 3, 30
molested, 14
mom, 8, 14

Index

moments, 1
money, 8, 13
mother, 3, 7, 8, 9, 10, 11, 13, 14, 15, 20
mountain, 1
mouth, 4
mustard seed, 2

N

naive, 14
nations, 18
natural mind, 20
night, 8, 10, 11, 17, 21
night hag, 17
nightmares, 16
noises, 17

O

obstacle, 18
Omega, 3
omnipotent, 30
omnipresent, 30
omniscience, 30
open streets, 12
overprotective parent, 8

P

pain, 18, 25
panic attacks, 16
parental rights, 20
Pastor, 28
patient, 29
perception, 33
perpetrator, 9
pervert, 7
physical abuse, 7
picture, 24
pills, 16
pimp, 8
plan, 12, 18, 31
police sirens, 16
possessive, 11
Post Traumatic Stress Disorder, 16
praying, 22
pregnancy, 11, 12
pregnant, 11, 12, 14, 15
presence, 26
principalities, 3
prison, 25
problem, 1, 22, 24

Index

promise keeper, 19
prophet, 18
pros, 28
prosper, 18
prostitution, 2, 10
psychiatric ward, 16
punish, 23, 32
purpose, 13, 19, 31

R

raped, 13
Raphael, 11
redeem, 10
relationship, 8, 22, 23, 25, 27, 28
Relationships, 24
repent, 19, 31
restraining order, 21
righteousness, 18, 19
rock, 11, 27
roller coaster ride, 20

S

satisfied, 5
scared, 8, 17

scarred, 32
sea, 1
Sebastian, 12
servants, 18
sex, 8, 10, 13, 22, 29
sexual abuse, 7, 23
sexual assault, 7
shoplifting, 10
sin, 23, 24, 26, 29
skin, 11
sleep, 17, 26
small still voice, 8
son, 11, 12, 19
spiritual realm, 17
Spiritual Russian Roulette, 23
spiritual wickedness, 3
stomach, 14
story, 2, 13, 18
strange town, 21
streets, 4, 32
strength, 27
suicide, 16, 33
surrendered, 29
survived, 6

T

Index

television, 17
testimony, 17
thankfulness, 33
thirsty, 6
time, 7, 8, 9, 10, 11, 12, 14, 16, 17, 18, 20, 22, 23, 25, 26, 27, 28, 29, 31
tongue, 4, 18
transparent, 27
trap set, 12
trauma, 33
turmoil, 20

U

unbelief, 20, 32
unforgiveness, 6
universe, 26
upstairs, 8

W

weakness, 13
weapon, 18
weaponry, 4
window, 8, 9

woman, 11, 17, 29
womb, 3, 17, 18
world, 3, 17
worthy, 30
wrestle, 3

Y

yawning, 14

www.ingramcontent.com/pod-product-compliance
Lightning Source LLC
Chambersburg PA
CBHW052125110526
44592CB00013B/1749